CONCEPTS IN SCIENCE

CURIE EDITION

CONSULTING SPECIALISTS IN THE SCIENCES

LAWRENCE P. EBLIN, *Chemistry*
Professor, Ohio University, Athens, Ohio
GARRETT HARDIN, *Biology and Ecology*
Professor, University of California, Santa Barbara
RICHARD C. LEWONTIN, *Biology and Genetics*
Professor, Harvard University, Cambridge, Massachusetts
ALISTAIR McCRONE, *Geology and Earth Science*
Professor, University of the Pacific, Stockton, California
FRANKLIN MILLER, JR., *Physics*
Chairman of Department, Kenyon College, Gambier, Ohio
FLETCHER G. WATSON, *Astronomy and Science Education*
Professor Emeritus, Harvard University, Cambridge, Massachusetts

THE AUTHORS

PAUL F. BRANDWEIN
Consultant to Schools on Curriculum and Instruction
Adjunct Professor, University of Pittsburgh
ELIZABETH K. COOPER
formerly Director of Elementary Education
Santa Monica, California
PAUL E. BLACKWOOD
Chief, Southeast Program Operations Branch
U.S. Office of Education*
MARGARET COTTOM-WINSLOW
Director of Curriculum, ICEA
New York, New York
JOHN A. BOESCHEN
formerly Science Teacher
Pinole, California
MORSLEY G. GIDDINGS
Professor of Education
Brooklyn College, City University of New York
FRANK ROMERO
Coordinator, Dallas Independent School District
Dallas, Texas
ARTHUR A. CARIN
Professor of Elementary and Early Childhood Education
Queens College, City University of New York

*The work of Paul Blackwood on the *Concepts in Science* Series was
done in his private capacity, and no official endorsement by the
U.S. Office of Education is intended or should be inferred.

**This series is dedicated to Marie Curie, one of the great
and noble scientists of the world.**

RED

CONCEPTS IN SCIENCE

CURIE EDITION

Paul F. Brandwein

Elizabeth K. Cooper

Paul E. Blackwood

Margaret Cottom-Winslow

John A. Boeschen

Morsley G. Giddings

Frank Romero

Arthur A. Carin

HARCOURT BRACE JOVANOVICH
New York Chicago San Francisco Atlanta Dallas *and* London

COVER: Runk/Schoenberger, Grant Heilman

HALF-TITLE PAGE: Roger Tory Peterson, Photo Researchers.

ILLUSTRATORS: Joseph Cellini, Felix Cooper, Graphic Arts International, Dick Morrill, Inc., Judy Skorpil, Bill Steinel.

PHOTOGRAPHERS: Oscar Buitrago, Glyn Cloyd, Eric Maristany, Erik Arnesen, Richard Watherwax, James Theologos, Robin Forbes, Padraic Cooper, George T. Resch, Jacques Jangoux.

PICTURE ACKNOWLEDGMENTS

Key: (t) top, (b) bottom, (l) left, (r) right, (c) center.

HBJ PHOTOS   Pages vi, 1, 2, 4, 6, 7, 8, 9, 10, 11, 12, 13, 14, 15, 16, 17, 18 (b), 19, 20 (t), 21 (t), 22, 26, 27, 28, 29 (br), 31, 32, 35, 36 (cr), 37 (t), 41, 43, 47, 60 (b), 66, 68, 69, 70, 71, 72, 73, 74, 75, 76, 77, 78, 79, 80, 81, 82, 83, 84, 85, 86, 87, 88, 89, 90, 91 (t) (cl), 94 (tr) (bl), 96 (b), 102, 103, 110, 111, 112 (tl), 113, 114 (br), 115 (b), 116, 117, 118 (b), 119, 121, 123, 124 (tl) (b), 125, 126, 131, 132 (b), 133 (c), 134, 143, 146 (br), 148, 149, 150, 151, 152, 153, 154, 155, 156, 157 (tl) (tr), 158, 159, 160, 161, 162, 163, 164, 165, 166, 167, 169, 170, 171, 172, 173, 174, 175, 176, 177, 180, 183, 185 (t) (cl) (cr).

RESEARCH PHOTOS   Pages 18: (t) Felix Cooper; (c) Dennis Simonetti, Taurus. 20: (b) Shostal. 21: (b) Peter Menzei, Stock Boston. 23: Felix Cooper. 25: Media Ltd. 29: (t) (c) (bl) Felix Cooper. 33: Frank Schreider, Photo Researchers. 34: (t) W. Stoy, Bruce Coleman; (b) Charles E. Schmidt, Taurus. 36: (cl) M. P. Kahl, Bruce Coleman; (tc) (tr) (bl) (cc) Felix Cooper. 37: (cr) Felix Cooper; (cl) Diane Rawson, Photo Researchers. 38: NASA. 48: J. R. Westlake, Jr., Taurus. 49: NASA. 50: NASA, UPI. 51: NASA. 52: Tim Kilby, DPI. 58: John Lutnes, Kitt Peak National Observatory. 59: © 1959 California Institute of Technology and Carnegie Institute of Washington, Hale Observatories. 60: (t) R. Oriti. 61: B. Wallis, Griffith Observatory. 62–63: NASA. 64: (cl) B. Wallis, Griffith Observatory; (cr) John Lutner, Kitt Peak National Observatory; (b) NASA. 65: NASA. 67: Felix Cooper. 91: (cr) Hal McKusick, DPI; (b) Felix Cooper. 92: Hermann Schlenker, Photo Researchers. 93: Kenneth W. Fink, Bruce Coleman. 94: (tl) Newfoundland and Labrador Tourist Development Office; (br) Malak, Annan Photo Features. 95: (t) Treat Davidson, National Audubon Society—Photo Researchers; (b) Allan Power, Bruce Coleman. 96 (tr) (tl) (tc)–97: Grant Heilman. 98: (t) Hans Reinhard, Bruce Coleman; (b) Grant Heilman. 99: (t) A. A. Francesconi, National Audubon Society—Photo Researchers; (b) Leonard Lee Rue III, Bruce Coleman. 100: Jane Burton, Bruce Coleman. 101: (tl) (tr) (bl) Alexander Klots; (br) Dr. E. R. Degginger, Bruce Coleman. 104: F. B. Grunzweig, Photo Researchers. 105: (t) Bucky Reeves, National Audubon Society—Photo Researchers; (b) Syd Greenberg, Photo Researchers. 106: (all) J. A. L. Cooke. 107: (both) Shell Oil Co. 108: (all) Jerome Wexler, Visual Teaching. 112: (tr) Dr. E. R. Degginger, Bruce Coleman. 114: (tr) Allan Power, Bruce Coleman; (c) Grant Heilman; (bl) Kenneth W. Fink, Bruce Coleman. 115: (t) Raymond Mendez; (cl) Alexander Klots; (cr) Grant Heilman. 118: (t) Ronald F. Thomas, Taurus. 120: R. N. Mariscal, Bruce Coleman. 122: Willis Peterson. 124: (tr) Owen Franken, Stock Boston. 127: (t) Roger Tory Peterson, Photo Researchers; (c) Tom McHugh, Photo Researchers; (b) M. Freeman, Bruce Coleman. 128: (t) Tom McHugh, Photo Researchers—Dallas Aquarium; (c) A. W. Ambler, National Audubon Society—Photo Researchers; (b) C. B. Frith, Bruce Coleman. 129: (tl) Hans Reinhard, Bruce Coleman; (tr) Stephen Dalton, Photo Researchers; (b) David Overcash, Bruce Coleman. 130: Bruce Coleman. 132: (t) David Overcash, Bruce Coleman; (c) Ronald Thomas, Taurus. 133: (t) Owen Franken, Stock Boston; (b) © 1976 Smithsonian Institution. 137: Rare Book Division, The New York Public Library; Astor, Lenox and Tilden Foundations. 138: California Department of Fish and Game. 139: Tom McHugh, Photo Researchers. 140: (both) G. Harrison, Bruce Coleman. 141: (both) Herb Taylor, Editorial Photocolor Archives. 142: G. R. Roberts. 144: (t) Bob Campbell, Bruce Coleman; (b) Norman Myers, Bruce Coleman. 145: (t) Marc & Evelyne Bernheim, Woodfin Camp; (b) Des Bartlett, Bruce Coleman. 146: (tr) Tom McHugh, Photo Researchers; (tl) Des Bartlett, Bruce Coleman; (bl) William R. Curtsinger, Photo Researchers. 147: (tl) Peter Kaplan, Photo Researchers; (tr) Joe Munroe, Photo Researchers; (tc) Simon Trevor, Bruce Coleman; (cl) Jen and Des Bartlett, Bruce Coleman; (cr) Simon Trevor, Bruce Coleman; (b) S. Nagendra, Photo Researchers. 157: (bl) Marc & Evelyne Bernheim, Woodfin Camp; (br) Jacques Jangoux. 185: (b) R. Carr. Bruce Coleman.

ISBN 0-15-365733-2   PRINTED IN THE UNITED STATES OF AMERICA

Contents

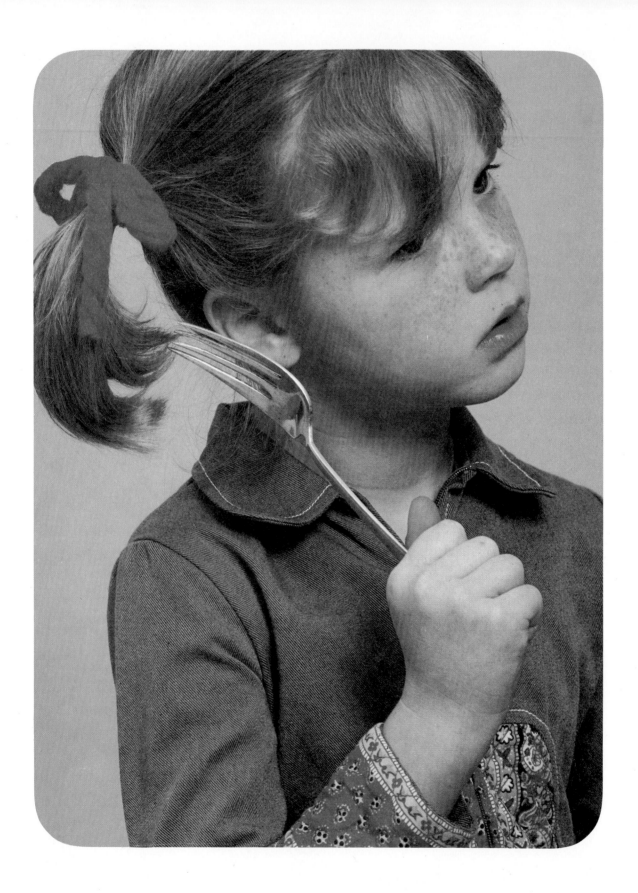

Silence
and Sound

Tap a fork on a table.

Hold the fork near your ear.

You will hear a sound!

How can a fork make a sound?

Let's find out.

Investigate

What we use ▶

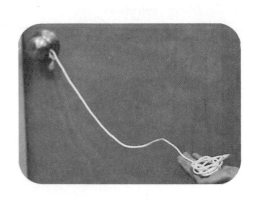

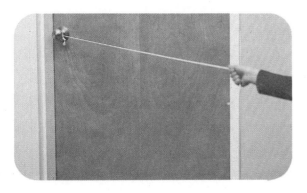

Pull the string tight.

Pull it down a little,
then let go.

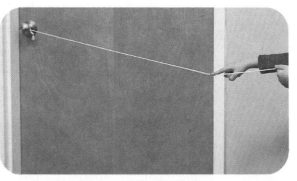

What does the string do?

What do you hear?

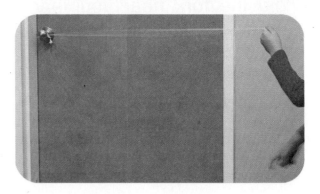

The string moves.

It moves up and down, like this.

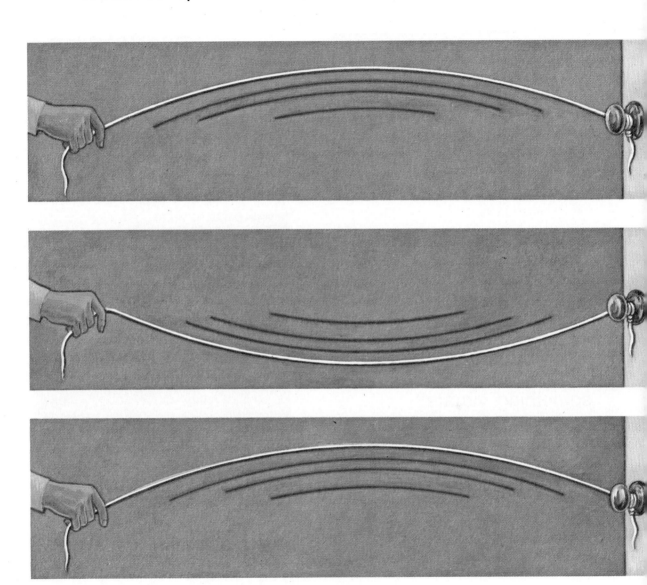

It vibrates.

The string vibrates.

You hear a sound.

Make some more sounds.

Can you feel

something vibrate?

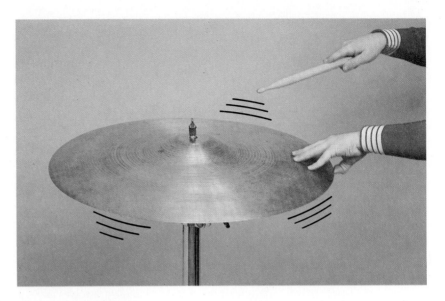

The cymbal vibrates.

The bell vibrates.

The drum vibrates.

Remember the fork?

Does the fork vibrate?

Make things that make sounds.

How do you make them vibrate?

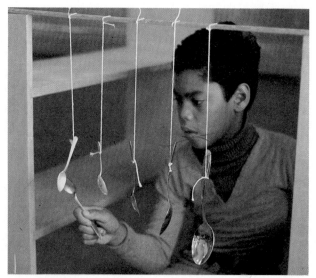

Carl calls to Tom.

Tom hears him.

How does the sound go from Carl to Tom?

Let's see.

Throw a stone
into the water.

It makes waves
in the water.

What do the
waves do?

Make a sound.

It makes waves
in the air.

What do the
waves do?

Carl calls Tom.

The sound waves spread out in the air.

How does Tom know when the sound waves reach him?

His ears let him know
about the sound waves.

You know sound can travel through air.

Your ears let you know.

Do you think sound can travel through wood?

Your ears will let you know.

Investigate!

Investigate

◀ *What we use*

Tap the table gently.

Listen.

> Do you hear
> the sound?

Now put your ear on the table.

Tap the table gently.

> Do you hear
> the sound now?

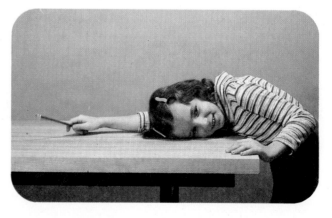

What do you think is happening now?

You hear
the sound waves
traveling through
the air.

Now you hear
the sound waves
traveling through
the wood.

Sound waves can travel
through water, too.

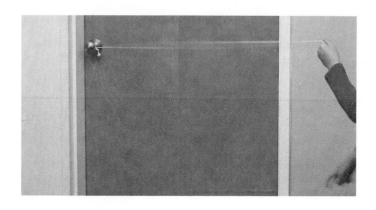

To make a sound,

something must vibrate.

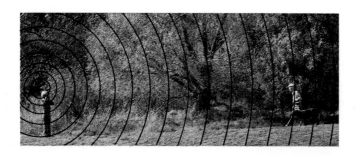

Sound travels in waves.

Sound waves

travel through air.

Sound waves

travel through wood.

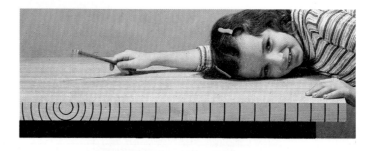

Sound waves

travel through water.

Suppose there is no air in this jar.

Could you hear the clock tick?

Could you hear the alarm go off?

Which rubber band is making a sound?

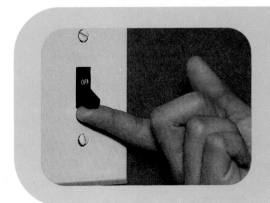

How many ways do you get light?

Darkness and Light

This is an old lamp.

It was used for light a hundred years ago.

Where is the light coming from?

What is giving off light?

What is burning?

Natural gas is a fuel.

Wood and coal are fuels.

Oil and candle wax are fuels, too.

We get light when fuel burns.

We get heat too.

Electricity

lights your home

at night.

What lights up

the streets

after dark?

Turn the crank.

Turn it fast.

As you turn,
you get electricity.

What is the electricity
doing?

This big machine
lights the bulbs
of a whole town.

What comes
from this machine?

Investigate

◀ *What we use*

Take a flashlight apart.

Find the bulb.

Find the switch.

Find the dry cells.

What makes the bulb light up?

How does the bulb make light?

The bulb has a
tiny wire in it.

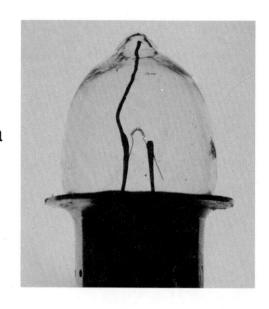

Electricity goes through

the wire.

The wire gets hot.

The wire gets very hot.

It gives off bright light.

How tiny the stars look!

But stars are not tiny.

Some are as big as the Sun.

Some are bigger than the Sun.

Then why do they look so small?

The Sun is a star.

We get light from the Sun.

Why do we get more light from the Sun
than from the other stars?

Does the light shine on the girl?

Does the light bend around the corner?

Why do you say so?

What we use ▶

The light travels in a straight line.

What happens when the light hits the mirror?

Why do you say so?

Investigate

What we use ▶

Look into
the mirror.

Do you see
the flashlight?

How does the
mirror work?

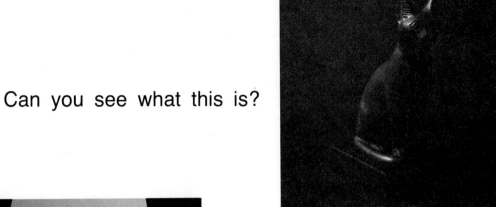

Can you see what this is?

Can you see what it is now?

Why?

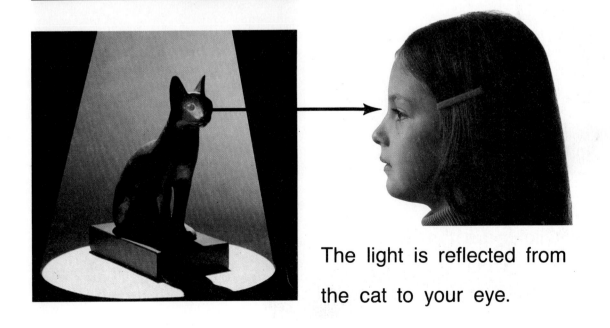

The light is reflected from
the cat to your eye.

What lights up the Moon?

What makes moonlight?

Does the light go through the hands?

How are the shadows made?

What we use ▶

Find things that light goes through.

Find things that no light goes through.

Find things that a little light goes through.

Which make the darkest shadows?

Why?

Did you ever see a rainbow?

Where?

What do you think makes a rainbow?

Drops of water
and sunlight
make a rainbow.

Each drop of water
makes colors
out of sunlight.

Investigate

◄ *What we use*

Let sunlight
go through
the prism.

What colors
do you see?

Red, orange, yellow, green, blue, violet?

Does a rainbow have all these colors?

one more time

We get light and heat
from fuels and electricity.

Most of our light and heat
comes from the Sun.

We see a thing
when it reflects light.

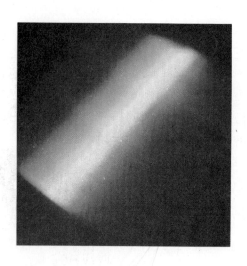

Sunlight is made up
of many colors.

Is candle wax
a fuel?

Suppose this cat reflected no light.
Could you see it?

There is no water
in the air here.
Can there be a rainbow?

Do they move?
Why do you think so?

Earth
and Its Space

This is where you live.

It is out in space.

It is moving.

It is moving while you read this.

Let's see how.

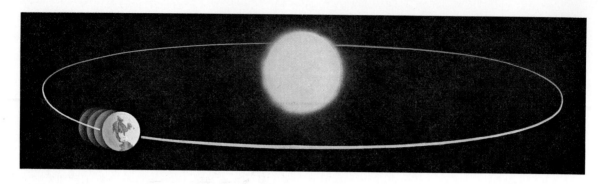

The Earth moves around the Sun.

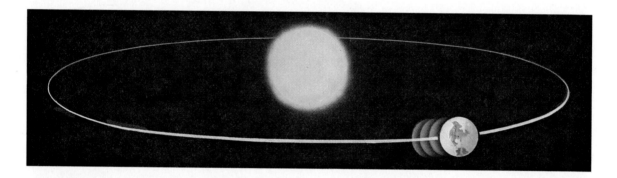

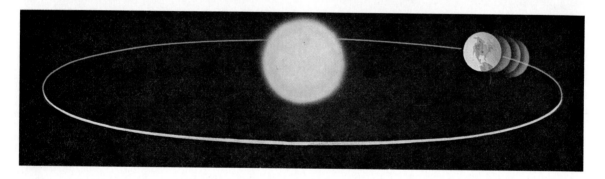

The Earth revolves around the Sun.

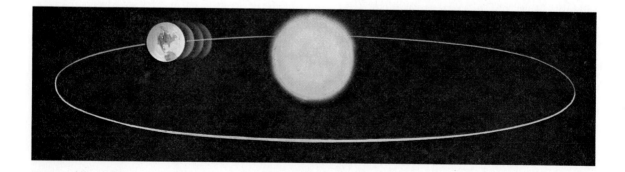

Investigate

What we use ▶

Show how the Earth revolves around the Sun.

The Earth turns around and around, like a top.
It rotates.

It rotates as it revolves around the Sun.

Investigate

What we use ▶

Show how the Earth rotates.

Show how the Earth revolves around the Sun.

The Earth is a planet.

There are eight other planets.

All of these planets revolve around the Sun.

The Moon revolves around the Earth.

The same side of the Moon is always
toward the Earth.

Investigate

◄ *What we use*

Show how
the Moon revolves
around the Earth.

This is the side of the Moon we see from Earth.

This side is always toward the Earth.

What do you see on this side of the Moon?

This is on the side of the Moon we cannot see
from Earth.

How was this photo taken?

Two astronauts landed on the Moon.

They set up some science experiments.

They set up the Moon rover.

Then they went for a ride in the rover.

They picked up soil and rocks.

They took pictures of hills and craters.

Where are the stars?

Are they near or far away?

What are stars like?

The Sun is the star nearest to the Earth.

We know what the Sun is like.

What does the Sun give off?

Long ago, people watched the stars.

The stars seemed to make pictures in the sky.

The people gave names to the star pictures.

What star picture can you find?

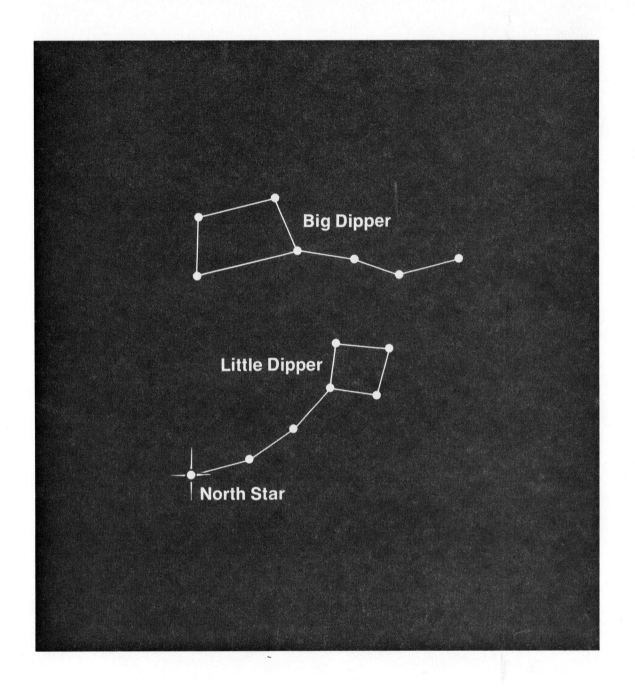

Find the Big Dipper.

Find the Little Dipper.

What else can you find?

It happened more than three hundred years ago.

Galileo made a telescope.

He watched the sky at night through it.

Galileo looked at the Moon.

It had mountains!

Saturn seemed to have ears.

What do you think the ears really were?

Jupiter had moons going around it!

This scientist is an astronomer.

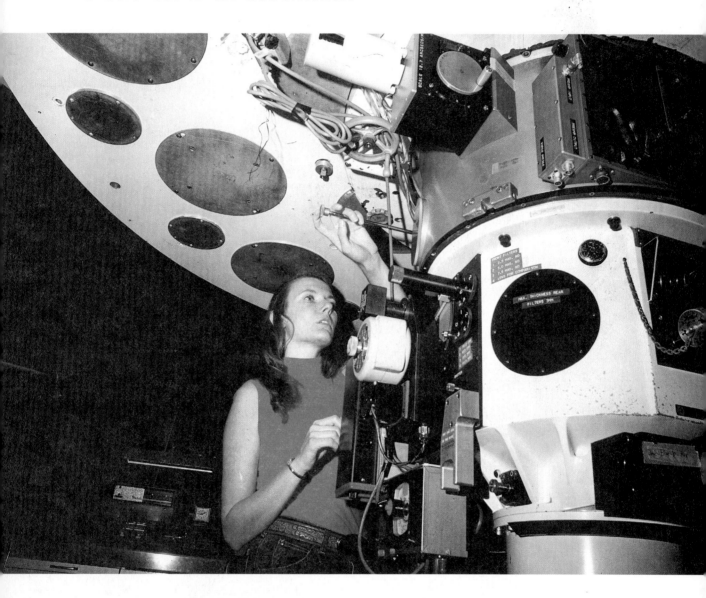

She studies the sky.

She studies things out in space.

This is an observatory.

Astronomers work here.

What do astronomers observe?

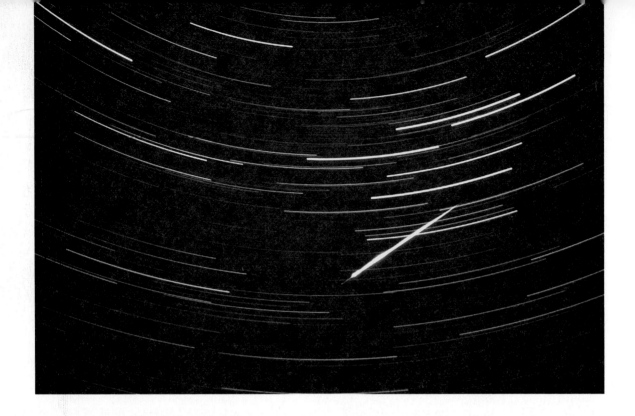

A light shoots across the night sky.

It looks like a falling star.

It is a meteor.

Most meteors burn up
high in the air.

This meteor hit the Earth
before all of it burned up.

A comet is much larger than a meteor.

It is lit by the Sun.

It revolves around the Sun.

What else revolves around the Sun?

A rocket blasts off.

It lifts a machine
into space.

The machine
goes into orbit
around the Earth.

It becomes a satellite.

Different satellites
do different things.

Telstar sends television programs.

In Skylab people live and work in space.

Some satellites watch the weather.

Others send pictures of things in space.

one more time

Planets move in orbits around the Sun.

In space nothing is still.

Comets and meteors move, too.

Every day we observe things in space.

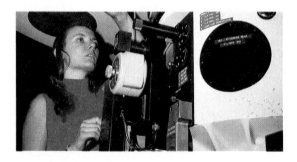

We send people and machines into space.

We are finding out more about space and about Earth.

Saturn

Mars

Which revolves around the Earth?

Which revolve around the Sun?

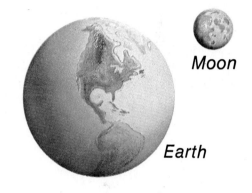

Moon

Earth

Venus

Which has plants and animals?

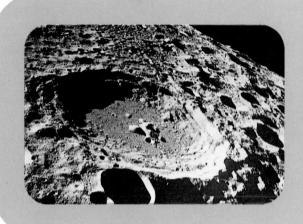

Why do you think there are no plants on the Moon?

Plants– Alive and Growing

Have you ever seen this plant?

Of course you have.

It is grass.

Grass grows in all sorts of places, doesn't it?

Let's see how!

If you don't cut it,
grass grows up.

It makes seeds.

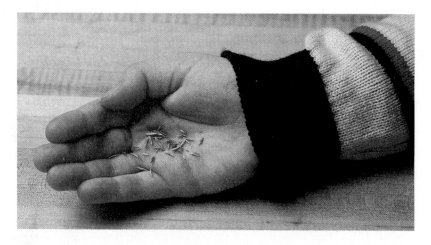

What we use ▶

Plant some grass seeds.

What do they need?

Investigate

What we use ▶

Put the seeds on wet cotton.

Next day open the seeds.

Look inside.

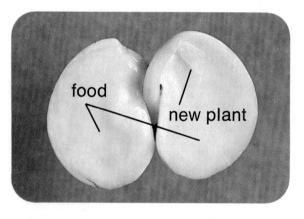

Can you find a new plant
in a bean seed?

Can you find the food
in a bean seed?

What can you find in
a corn seed?

This plant grew
from a bean seed.

This plant grew
from a corn seed.

One of these plants is a kind of grass.

Which do you think it is?

One plant was watered every day.

The other was not watered.

Which plant needs water?

Why do you say so?

Investigate

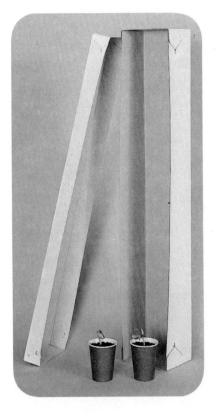

◀ *What we use*

Keep one bean plant in the sunlight.

Put the other bean plant in the dark.

Water both plants every day.

What do these plants need besides water?

73

◄ *What we use*

Put two seeds in each jar.

Keep the seeds wet.

Put one jar

in a cold, dark place.

Put the other jar

in a warm, dark place.

Which seeds sprout and grow into plants?

What do these seeds need?

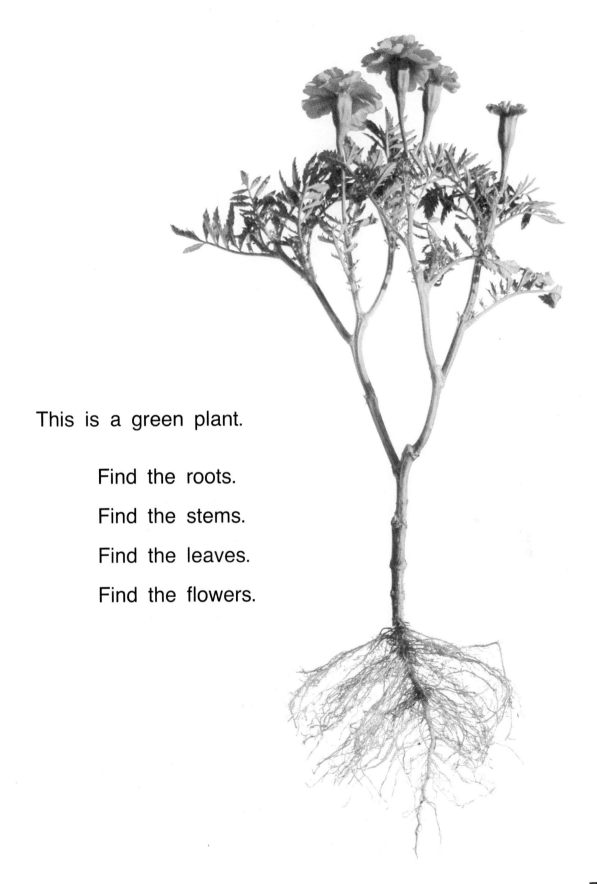

This is a green plant.

Find the roots.

Find the stems.

Find the leaves.

Find the flowers.

What we use ▶

Did these roots
grow down or up?

How do you know?

76

Roots

take in water

from the soil.

The water

travels up

the roots.

It goes to

the rest of

the plant.

◀ *What we use*

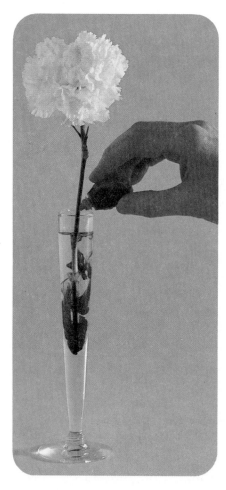

What happened
to the flower?

Why?

Try other flowers.

Try other colors.

A green plant needs food.

It makes food in its leaves.

It uses sunlight to make its food.

What does it do with its food?

flower   fruit   seeds

flower   fruit   seeds

flower   fruit   seeds

Some plants have flowers.

A fruit grows from part of the flower.

What grows inside the fruit?

Investigate

What we use ▶

Look inside a cone.

Take a cone apart.

Take off the scales.

Take out the seeds.

What can grow
from the seeds?

It is spring.

The peach tree has flowers.

What comes to the flowers?

What grows after the flowers fall?

What grows inside each peach?

What happens when a pit is planted?

A fir seed falls from a cone.

It falls on moist soil.

What happens to the seed?

Why?

The Sun shines

on the young fir tree.

How does the tree

get water?

The small fir tree grows.

What does it need?

Where do
the seeds grow?

What can grow
from the seeds?

Investigate

What we use ▶

Put the lemon in the dish.

Put the dish in the plastic bag.

Tie the bag tightly.

Put the bag in a warm, dark place.

Keep it there for a week or more.

What grows on the lemon?

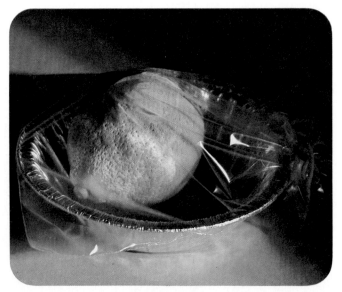

86

Molds are tiny plants.

The mold plants
get their food
from what
they grow on.

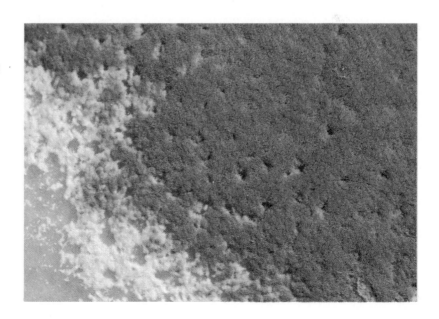

What roots do we eat?

What leaves and stems do we eat?

We eat flowers too.

What flowers do we eat?

What seeds do we eat?

What fruits do we eat?

one more time

Most green plants grow from seeds.

Green plants need air, water, light, and soil.

Green plants use light to make food in their leaves.

We depend on food made by green plants.

why do you say so

apple

corn

bean

What kind of plant can grow
from each seed?

Which will be trees?

What is made in the leaves?

What do the roots do?

Could we live
without plants?

What does this animal need
to live and grow?

Animals–
Alive and Growing

Here you see an animal and a plant.

You know what the plant needs.

Does the animal need the same things?

What can the plant do that the animal can't do?

What can the animal do that the plant can't do?

What kinds of fish do you eat?

Where do fish live?

What do they eat?

Big fish eat small fish.

Small fish eat smaller fish.

The smallest fish eat
tiny animals and plants.

The tiny animals eat
tiny green plants.

How do the
tiny green plants
get food?

Jersey

Holstein

These cows are dairy cows.

They give lots of milk.

What do dairy cows eat?

Guernsey

What foods are made

from milk?

Cows eat grass.

They eat
other green plants.

They eat hay.

What do they
use their food for?

This is
a rooster.

This is
a hen.

Which one
lays eggs?

What do chickens eat?

What do
squirrels eat?

Where does their food come from?

A butterfly dips its tongue into a flower.

It uses its tongue like a drinking straw.

What do butterflies get from flowers?

A butterfly lays eggs.

What hatches from the eggs?

How do caterpillars get food?

How do caterpillars change?

What we use ▶

Keep an insect
or other small animal
for a day.

What will
the animal need?

Take care
of the animal.

Watch it.

Then let it go free.

Put a piece of potato in with the animal.

Will it eat potato?

Will it eat a piece of banana?

Does it like darkness or light?

Watch and
find out.

What has the spider caught?

What will the spider do with it?

The black widow
is a poisonous spider.

It makes a cocoon
for its eggs.

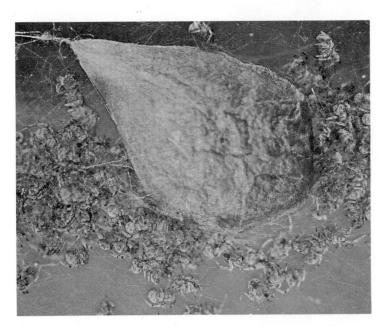

Young black widows
leave the cocoon.

Each goes off
to hunt for food.

NEVER touch a black widow spider. Why?

A starfish lays eggs.

A larva hatches
from a starfish egg.

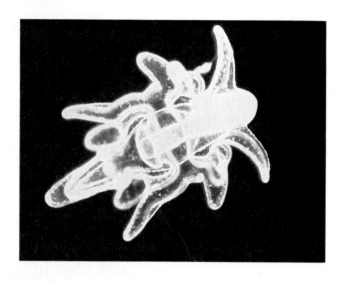

The larva changes
and grows rays.

How does
the starfish
use its rays?

The starfish moves along on its rays.

It puts its rays around a scallop.

It pulls and pulls to open the shell.

Then what does the starfish do?

A ladybug lays eggs.

Grubs hatch from the eggs.

The grubs change to adults.

What will

the adults eat?

Adult ladybugs eat insects.

Some orange and lemon trees were dying.

Insects were killing them.

Ladybugs were used to save the trees.

What did the ladybugs do?

What we use ▶

Watch
an earthworm.

Feel its
soft body.

Find out
how it moves.

What does the earthworm need to live?

Fill a box or tank with soil.

Keep it in a cool place.

Put in bits of lettuce and cereal.

Put in some earthworms.

Keep the soil damp but not muddy.

Find out how

earthworms live.

Find out how they make the soil better.

Green plants grow in sunlight.

They use light from the Sun to make food.

What are
these animals
eating?

Where does
their food
come from?

What foods do we get from plants?

What foods do we get from animals?

Could we have food if there were no
green plants?

Could we have food if the Sun did not shine?

one more time

Animals and plants are living things.

They grow.

They need food.

And so do we.

Green plants use sunlight to grow.

Animals use food
that is made by green plants.

And so do we.

Animals need food.

They need food from green plants.

And so do we.

What would happen if a caterpillar had no green plants?

What will happen to—

the insects on this plant?

the plant?

the ladybug?

Suppose green plants stopped using light from the Sun. Would it matter?

How would you care for this plant?

Caring for Plants and Animals

The Earth has many green plants.

Why is it good to live
where green plants grow?

How can we take care of Earth's plants?

What can you do to help?

Some
pond plants
grow under
the water.

Some have roots in the bottom of the pond
and flowers and leaves on top of the water.

Many kinds
of plants
grow
in the sea.

Make a garden
for pond plants.

Use a big,
clean jar.

Use clean sand and water.

Put in some aquarium plants.

Put in pond snails and small fish.

Keep the garden in a cool, light place.

Why does it need light?

Desert plants get very little water.

Some can store water.

Some have long roots that go far to get water.

What would happen to these plants if
the desert never had rain?

Make a garden
for desert plants.

Put in sandy soil and
a few small rocks.

Put the desert plants
in the sandy soil.

Wear gloves when you
plant a cactus.

Keep the desert garden
in a dry, sunny place.

Water it lightly
every few weeks.

These ferns grow well in the shade.

So do other small plants.

They grow well in the cool, wet woods.

What if many trees are cut down?

What will happen to the small plants?

Make a home for plants from the woods.

Put in some pebbles.

Put sand on top of the pebbles.

Put peat moss and soil on top of the sand.

Put in small rocks and bits of old wood.

Put in plants that grow well
in wet, shady places.

Water the soil.

Put on the cover.

Many kinds of plants
grow in cities.

What do city plants need?

Who takes care of them?

What plants
can you find
on your street?

Is it good
to have plants
around us?

Why?

Investigate

What we use ▶

Fill a pan with soil.

Plant seeds in rows.

Water the garden.

Put the garden
in a sunny place.

Keep soil damp
but not muddy.

If the plants look crowded,
pull some out.

What plants
do you
want to grow?

The Earth has many animals.

What do they need to stay alive?

What can you do to help?

These animals
live on land.

Can you name them?

Animals move around
to get food.

What else
do animals need?

Some animals
live in water.

Do you know
these animals?

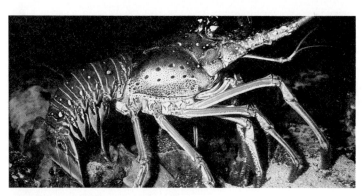

What do
these animals
need to live?

Some animals can fly.

Name these animals.

How does flying help these animals stay alive?

These are wild guinea pigs.

They live in South America.

They eat grass and other plants.

They make their homes in the ground.

This is a tame guinea pig.

How would you take care of it?

What would you do —

    to keep it alive?

    to keep it growing well?

    to keep it safe?

one more time

Plants and animals
live on land
and in the air.

When land and air change,
some plants and animals die.

Plants and animals live in water.

When the water changes,
some of them die.

People can clean up
Earth's land and air.

People can clean up
Earth's water.

Then plants and animals
can live.

And so can we.

**why
do you
say so
?**

Do these plants
need care?

Does this
make any difference
to animals?

You will never see
this bird alive.

Can you guess why?

Caring About Living Things

This is a dodo.

Many years ago sailors came in ships.

They came to islands where the dodos lived.

The dodos could not fly.

Their wings were too small.

Sailors killed dodos.

More people came.

They killed more dodos.

The animals they brought ate dodo eggs.

But one man took a dodo back home with him.

Some people made paintings of dodos.

Some wrote down what the dodos were like.

So you can see a model in a museum.

You can see some old drawings and paintings.

But you will never see a living dodo.

They were all killed.

The dodos are gone forever.

Great herds of these elk once lived in California.

But people made towns and farms in the valleys.

Hunters shot the elk for meat and hides.

Farmers shot the elk to get rid of them.

The elk were in danger of disappearing forever.

Like the dodos.

At last only a few elk were left.

One farmer let them live on his land.

Then a new law was passed.

No one was allowed to kill these elk.

The herds grew bigger. The elk were saved.

They have not disappeared.

This man is catching
lobsters for food.

The lobsters are caught
in lobster pots.

Once the lobster walks in,
it can't get out.

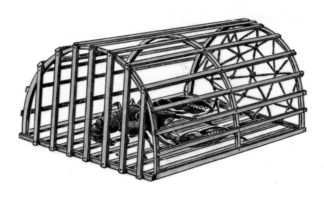

People used to catch
many lobsters.

But now there are few lobsters
in the pots.

What do you think could be
the reason?

Too many lobsters have been caught.

Not enough lobsters are being born.

So people are trying to save the lobsters.

They raise millions of tiny lobsters.

They set them free in the ocean, to grow up.

With our help,
lobsters will not
disappear.

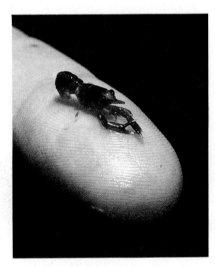

These plants
are cycads.

Once there were
great forests
of cycads.

They grew
in most parts
of the Earth.

Then the cycads
began to die out.

No one knows
just why.

Today they
live in only
a few places.

But cycads are being saved.

Today, people plant cycads.

Cycads need a warm, moist place.

They grow well indoors, in pots.

Their seeds sprout and grow easily.

Look for cycads in plant stores and
greenhouses.

Elephants live where green plants grow.

They need much food to stay alive.

Years ago, many elephants lived in Africa.

But some were killed for food.

Some were killed for their ivory tusks.

And some were killed for sport.

The land is changing
in Africa.

Villages and farms
are spreading out.

There is less and less
room for elephants.

They are in danger of disappearing forever.

But people are trying
to save them.

How do you think
they may be saved?

The elk
in California
have been saved.

People are trying
to save elephants
in Africa . . .

lobsters in the
Atlantic Ocean . . .

and cycads.

why do you say so

These plants and animals still live on Earth.

But they are in danger of disappearing.

Should they be saved?

Plants and animals need food.

Do you need food?

Why?

The Energy You Use

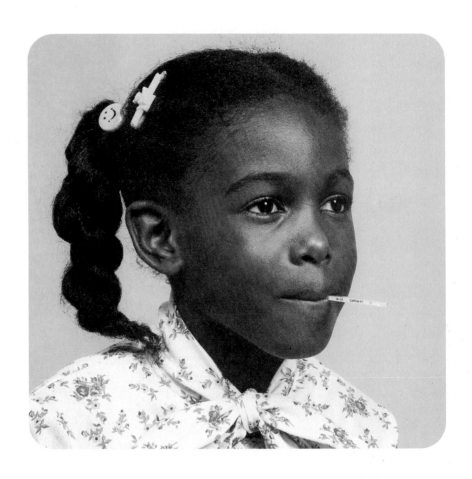

Breathe gently into your hands.

Is your breath warm or cold?

Take your temperature.

Is your body warm or cold?

The thermometer shows that your body is warm.

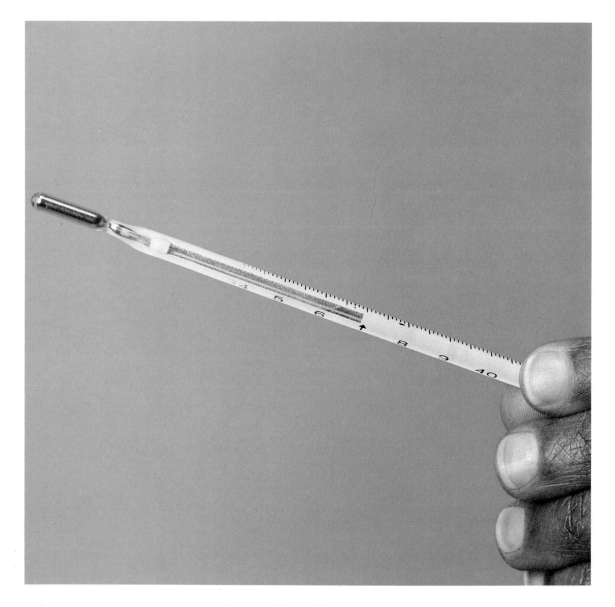

What makes your body so warm?

Let's investigate.

What we use ▶

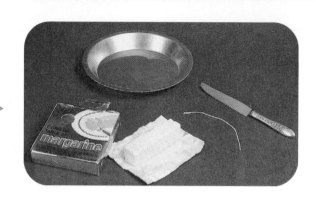

Make a margarine candle.

Use hard, cold margarine.

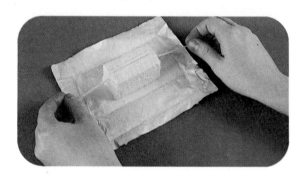

Use a string for a wick.

Rub some margarine on the top end of the wick.

Stand the candle in a metal pan.

Let your teacher light the candle.

Where does the heat come from?

The margarine is burning. It gives off heat.

Margarine burns because it has energy.

When you eat margarine you get energy.

You get energy from other foods too.

You turn some energy into heat.

The heat makes you warm.

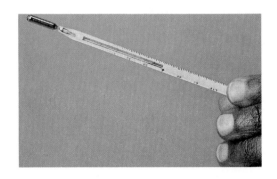

It takes energy to play.

How do you use energy?

It takes energy to
work.

Have you ever been sick?
It takes energy to get well.

How do you save energy
when you are sick?

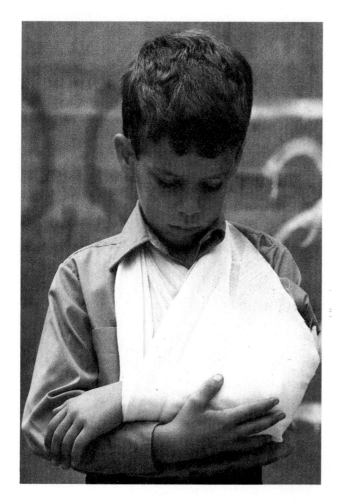

It takes energy to fix
a broken bone.

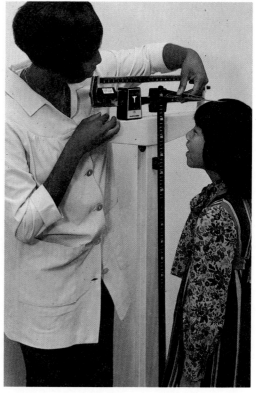

Does it take energy to grow?

Where do you get energy
for the things your body does?

Investigate

What we use ▶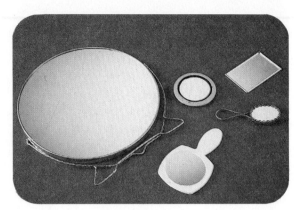

How are you and your friends alike?

How are you different?

Do you and your friends use energy?

How do you get it?

They live in different countries.

Do they grow? Do they play?

Greece

Mexico

Liberia

Japan

Do they need energy?

How do they get energy?

In what other ways are they like you?

one more time

Your body
uses energy
to keep warm.

It uses energy
to work and play.

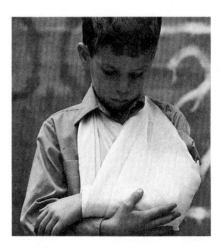

It uses energy to grow and change.
It uses energy to heal and repair.

The energy you use comes from food.

You eat because
you need energy.

why do you say so ?

Which takes more energy?

Does it take
energy
to do this?

Do you know when you
need energy?

Put some sugar in water.

Stir it.

Where does the sugar go?

The Matter You Use

Close your eyes.

Don't touch.

Don't taste.

Which is soap?

Which is an orange?

How can you tell?

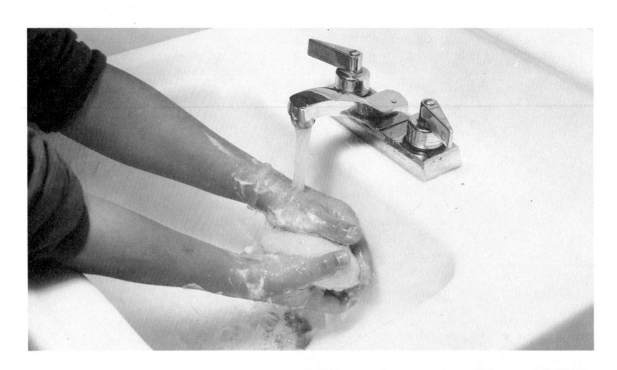

You know what these are.

They are pieces of matter.

Why can you smell them?

Let's see.

Tiny bits leave the soap.

The bits are too small to be seen.

Some bits get to your nose.

Then you can smell the soap.

Why can you smell the orange?

Investigate

What we use ▶

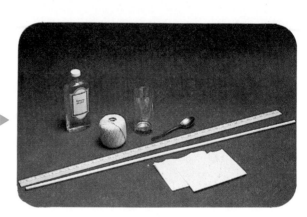

Take the cap off
the bottle of alcohol.

Can you smell alcohol?

Why?

Put a spoonful in the glass.

Balance the rod so that it is level.

Wet one paper with alcohol.

Put the wet paper on one end of the rod.

Put the dry paper on the other end.

What happens as the wet paper dries?

Why?

What we use ▶

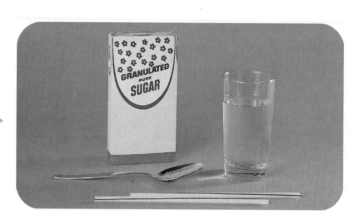

Put in four spoonfuls
of sugar.

Stir the water.

Watch what happens.

Keep on stirring!

What's happening to the bits of sugar?

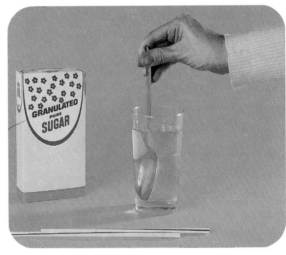

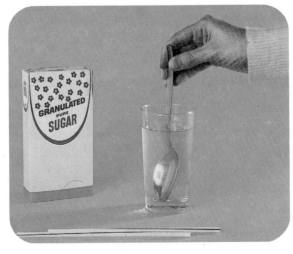

Are the bits of sugar still there?

How can you tell?

Here's what happens
to the sugar.

As you stir, the bits of
sugar come apart.

The bits keep on coming
apart.

They get smaller and smaller.

You can't see them.

After a while the bits of
sugar can't get any
smaller.

These bits are called molecules.

They are molecules of sugar.

Sugar has molecules.

Water has molecules, too.

Put some water
in a glass.

Let it stand.

One day later.

Two days later.

What happens to the water?

How does it happen?

You can't see a molecule of water.

But molecules of water jump into the air.

We say the water evaporates.

More and more molecules of water leave the glass.

After a while all the water is in the air.

It has all evaporated.

Put some water in a jar.

Put a lid on the jar.

Let it stand.

Will all the water evaporate?

Why?

What happens if you
take the lid off?

Why?

Try it!

The molecules of water can't get out.

Can the water evaporate now?

How?

The water going into the air
is a gas.

The gas has no shape
of its own.

The water in the dish is a liquid.

The liquid takes the shape
of whatever it is in.

Freeze the water.

Now it is a solid.

The solid has
its own shape.

one more time

You smell something.

Bits of matter
travel to your nose.

Bits of sugar break apart in water.

They become smaller and smaller.

The smallest bit of all
is a molecule of sugar.

Molecules of water jump into the air.

Water evaporates.

Sugar is matter. Water is matter. So is air.

Matter may be a solid,
a liquid, or a gas.

What will happen
to the water?

Could you smell it?

Is the sugar still there?

How can you tell if this water is
hot or cold—without touching it?

Heat and Change

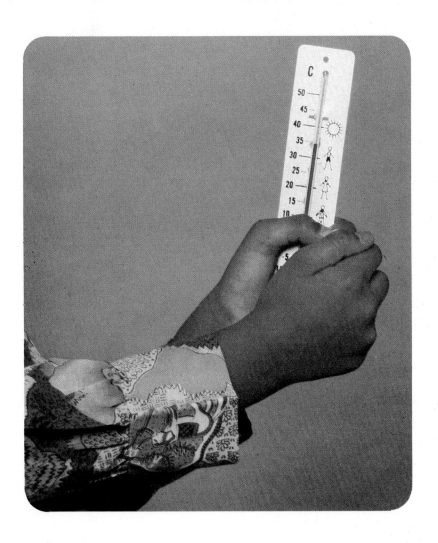

Put your hand on a thermometer.

Put it around the little glass bulb.

What happens to the red line?

Why?

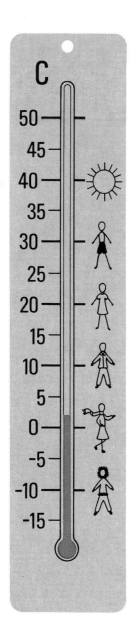

The thermometer is
a glass tube.

Inside the glass tube is
a red liquid.

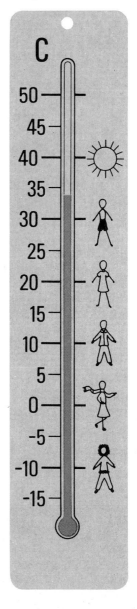

Your hand warms the liquid.

The liquid goes up in the tube.

Why?

Here's why the liquid goes up.

The liquid is made up of molecules.

When the liquid is heated,
the molecules move
away from each other.

The liquid takes up more room.

We say the liquid expands.

What we use ▶

Stretch the balloon
over the bottle.

Heat the water in the pot.

Put the bottle
in the hot water.

Why does the balloon
get bigger?

Molecules of air fill the bottle.

They fill the balloon, too.

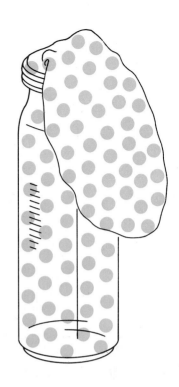

The air gets hot.

What happens
to the molecules?

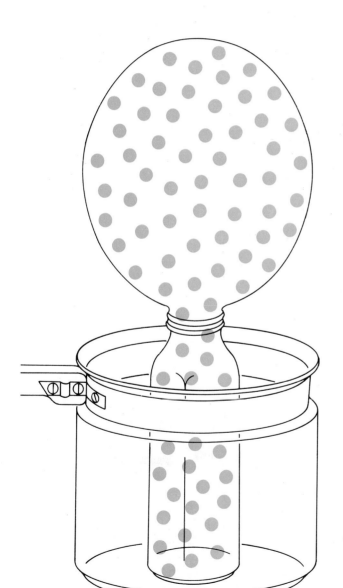

The molecules move away
from each other.

Heat makes
the air expand.

The balloon gets bigger.

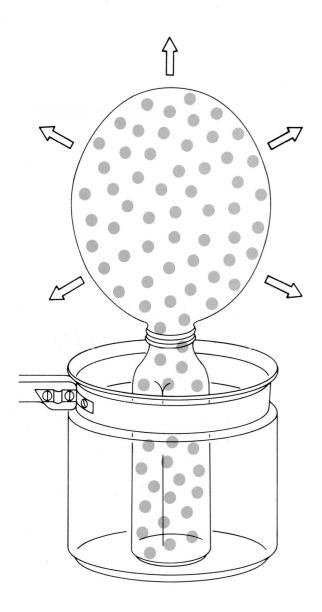

Air is made up of gases.

When the gases
are heated, they expand.

What would you do to make

the balloon small again?

Why?

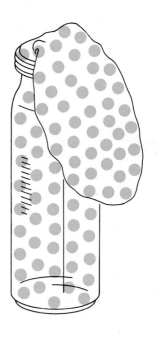

The metal cap won't come off.

It is too tight.

Hold it under hot water.

Now the cap comes off easily!

Why?

one more time

When the gases
are heated,
they expand.

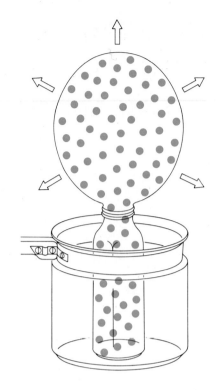

When the liquid
is heated,
it expands.

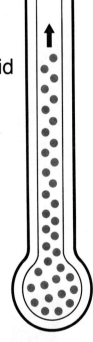

When the solid
is heated,
it expands.

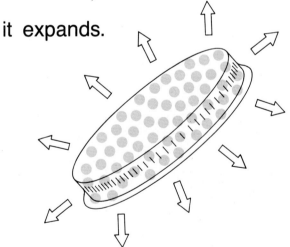

When the molecules are heated,
they move away from each other.

Will this balloon expand?

Where are the molecules moving farther away
from each other?

Will this horseshoe
be bigger when it cools?

Key Concept Terms

Use these terms when you talk about ideas in science.

B C D E F G H I J
9 0 1 2 3 4 5 6 7